A Black Brick in a White (Lego) System

Bhishma Asare

First published 2024
By Risky Publishing
34-35, Hatton Garden, London, England, EC1N 8DX
© 2024 Bhishma Asare

All rights reserved. No part of this book may be reprinted or reproduced or utilized in any form or by any electronic, mechanical, or other means, now known or hereafter invented, including photocopying or recording, or in any information storage or retrieval system, without permission in writing from the publishers.

ISBN 978-1-0686992-0-7

Asare, Bhishma.
      A Black Man Stuck in a White Education System / Bhishma Asare.
      p. cm.
Includes bibliographical references.

To my parents, and aunty Amma Opoku for your guidance.

Contents

1	Introduction	1
2	Methods and Methodology	5
3	School, Church, School	8
4	School, Church, School Analysis	17
5	Rap Therapy and NQT Teaching	29
6	Rap Therapy and NQT Teaching Analysis	37
7	Learning during Lockdown	42
8	Learning during Lockdown Analysis	51
9	A Trip to the Globe Theatre	55
10	A Trip to the Globe Theatre Analysis	57
11	Struggles	60
12	Discussion	63

Appendix 67

Bibliography 74

1 Introduction

Throughout my career in education, I came to notice very clearly that there was a lack of Black representation within the education sector. This lack of representation, which was made clear to me as my time developed as a Black male English teacher, indicated that there were problems not only within the curriculum but how other White teachers view and treat students of colour. These racial biases stem from multiple factors, which have been explored throughout this research project. This book not only aims to expose the racism within the education sector, but it is a reflective and auto ethnographical piece which explores different events and interactions throughout my life which all intersect. These experiences that have taken place are exclusive to my life and are reflective of one of my previous secondary schools, where I taught English. Although these experiences are exclusive to myself and reflective of my encounters in this London-based secondary school, the feelings throughout this research will be shared by many Black practitioners across the nation and possibly worldwide.

I reflect throughout this research on my own experiences growing up and interlink it with data captured from students, enabling me to understand the experiences of the young people whom I teach. I explore the needs for music within the classroom, in particular rap music and how it can be used as an effective tool amongst adolescents in communities full of rich culture, but extreme deprivation. The investigation not only delves deeper into students' work, but gives an account of how students often view rap music within the classroom and its need to break stereotypes in the education sector.

The aim of this research is not only to share my own experience, interlinking it to Critical Race Theory and the problems in conjunction with a racialised genre of music – rap, in the English classroom, but it is to permit other practitioners to reflect on their encounters with Black teachers and Black students and for them to take proactive steps in breaking the stigmatic nature of racism within education. The aims are also to point out the clear discrepancies of how both White and Black children are treated as students, alongside the differences in how I as a Black teacher have been treated differently within my department and wider, within my school; much of which stemmed from the management culture in my school, which trickled down to teacher level. I explore the problems in relation to the demographic of teachers within the UK education sector and their need to understand culture and socioeconomical problems within the institutes whereby they educate is vital. I argue that if teachers do not understand the above, it can be detrimental and will act as a disservice to the young people who need to formulate their own ideas and interpretations within education. I also speak on experiences that I had as a teacher and how rap was racialised through authority and hierarchy as the Head of Department, despite witnessing its impact instructed me to "stay on the scheme of work".

Initially, this research was to take a completely different form[1], whereby it would have been an exploration of how 'Music could be used in the English classroom, in conjunction with conversation to nurture the love of English amongst students.' This, however, could not be undertaken as the original research title was vetoed by those in charge at my previous school. This rejection led me to write an auto-ethnographical piece and explore the racial problems within

---

[1] See Appendix 1

education, such as why this original research title was not permitted by my school. It explores not only my blackness but explores how my cultural capital played a major part within the depths of my classroom, making me a likable teacher and one who understood the children; thus, causing jealousy and evidently mistreatment through racial bias and consequential actions.

When embarking on this research, my initial strategy was to read as much content as I could on racism in the education sector and delve into the history of oppression of Black people. When exploring this content deeply, I came to discover that in the UK, in comparison to the US, there appears to be a shortage of research into these issues alongside gender. It was very miniscule and the content which did exist, predominantly were written by women of colour, who were based in the United States of America; there was little to no content on this research done by men of colour, especially based in the United Kingdom. This exploration led me to discover that there was racism in not only education at a state-school level, but racism within academia and scholarship also. This discovery, motivated me to delve deeper into the reading that existed and with that coinciding with my own experience, I concluded that the lack of Black male academics writing pieces like this are at a deficit because of how tough the system is and the struggle seems like a never ending battle whereby many Black people are "tired of arguing with those White people" (Ladson-Billings, G, 1998, p.14). The literature which is used throughout the research, can be found in the *method and methodology* section, however although the reading referenced can be found throughout this piece of work, there are still problems that I have found within this scope of reading.

The problems which I have found throughout my research journey is that the scholars who have written very valid arguments, do not come from the lived experience of a Black man and this research helps to fill that gap. This is problematic because there is not enough representation in academia for me to pull resourcing from, meaning that my predominant support comes from the following at hindsight: a White man (David Gillborn), a Californian woman (Tara J. Yosso) and a Black woman (Gloria Ladson-Billings). With this being said, although perspective and argument is important and the support is welcomed and relevant, the lived experiences of Black males in education are quite difficult to discover in a world full of journals. I argue that there should be more Black male scholars, ones who despite understanding that the fight against inequality is an uphill battle, are resilient and forthcoming.

2 Methods and Methodology

In this research I have used autoethnography as the predominant writing method. I have chosen to use autoethnography because "historically, storytelling has been a kind of medicine to heal the wounds of pain caused by racial oppression" (Ladson-Billings, G, 1998, p.14) and throughout my experiences, this has acted as a therapeutic method to heal some of the "wounds of pain" (Ladson-Billings, G, 1998, p.14) caused throughout my traumatic experiences in the education system. Autoethnography deemed the best method to use for this research as it is much to do with personal experience, but the writing is heavily influenced by readings which I have researched located in Critical Race Theory and because I am informed by the models of autoethnography that I have read, this research does not follow a conventional social-sciences structure.

I like that autoethnography empowers the freedom and balance between creativity, telling the story as it is alongside using academics to support my argument. Thus, autoethnography also can act as an aid to anyone who is also facing similar hardship or situations and gives them an insight to understand that problems of the world are not exclusive to one person, but many can learn from one experience. This autoethnography doesn't only act as a supportive mechanism for the 'Black experience' in education, but it acts as an insightful tool which White scholars and educators can read in order to reflect on their current and future actions. This research also uses the form of reflection groups alongside individual reflection and interviews as this allowed me to capture the first-hand experience of Black children within the school and how they viewed elements of education such as English and the use of rap in the classroom.

Throughout this process, I have been influenced by Devika Chawla's autoethnography; *"Walk, Walking, Talking, Home"* (Chawla, D. 2013. p.162-172) in which she highlights her experiences of growing up and reluctantly going on daily walks with her grandmother. She speaks about her life and where she has come from alongside her schooling experiences. This autoethnography out of the many which I had come across such as *""Sit with Your Legs Closed!" and Other Sayin's from My Childhood"* (Boylorn, R. 2013. p.173-185) and *"Fire A Year in Poems"* (Weems, M. 2013. p. 313-320) resided with my own story and my own autoethnography and elements of Devika Chawla's autoethnography influenced my writing style. Alongside Devika Chawla, I was given much guidance as to what Critical Race Theory was and the depths of this study through readings such as (Gillborn, D. 2008) *"Racism and Education coincidence or conspiracy?"* in which he highlights issues within society in relation to race and systematic oppression, profoundly demonstrating about the gaps in education and the differences between White and Black attainment within the education sector. There are two additional academics who have had a significant influence on this research. The first academic is (Ladson-Billings, G, 1998) whose *"Just what is critical race theory and what's it doing in a nice field like education?"* highlights the inequalities in education but also a need to actively make changes within the system through representation and reflection. The second academic is (Yosso, T. 2005) whose *"Whose culture has capital? A critical race theory discussion of community cultural wealth"* explores community cultural wealth and so challenges the notion of "traditional interpretations of cultural

Methods and Methodology

capital" (Yosso, T. 2005. p.69); she further argues that although many people of colour come from poor backgrounds, they still have a vast amount of "cultural knowledge, skills and abilities" (Yosso, T. 2005. p.76) all of which should be used and not ignored.

3 School, Church, School

Music has always played a significant role in my life. For as long as I could remember, the sounds, the tempo, the lyrics that flow smoothly to an instrumental has been curative. In order for this account to make absolute sense, I need to take you back to my Year 4 class with Miss Devitta[2]. Miss Devitta was the only Black teacher in Babington School[3] at the time. It was 2001 and I was 9 years old, and Maths was always one of my weaker subjects at the time. Often distracted and talkative there was a lesson which changed my perspective on Maths completely which Miss Devitta had planned and captured my undivided attention. Miss Devitta was teaching the class the six times tables and all throughout the year I had struggled with multiplication and division. This lesson however was very different as Miss Devitta decided to teach us a rap to remember the six times tables which she got the whole class to rap together. 23 years later and I still remember the rap:

"6, 12, 18, 24, 30, 36
We now go onto the bigger numbers
42, 48, 54
60, 66 and 72

---

[2] All names of people in this research has been changed to a culturally appropriate pseudonym.
[3] The name of the school has been changed.

>And again
>6, 12, 18, 24, 30, 36
>We now go onto the bigger numbers
>42, 48, 54
>60, 66 and 72"

Although this rap was embedded into my mind 23 years ago, the very fact that I have remembered this rap for such a long period of time is an indication of how fundamental music, particularly rap has been in my life. We didn't rap to an instrumental backing track, but the way the words were pronounced created rhythm in itself that was memorable. This lesson was the first lesson where I was able to see how rap could help me throughout school and although I subliminally knew that this would be a useful tool, it wasn't until I reached secondary school that I started using this tool to help me get through and ultimately aid me to complete my GCSEs. Looking back to Year 4, I realise as an adult and English practitioner in the professional working world, that Miss Devitta was a great asset to the school. In saying this, she was the minority as she was the only Black teacher. I can only imagine that through teaching lessons differently through the merging of maths, English and music that she would have faced scrutinization by her colleagues and possibly some of the White parents. Up until this experience with Miss Devitta, I had faced my fair share of racism within the school from teachers.

My family background is significantly important and frames the basis of this autoethnography. My mother, Neina, is of Indian descent and moved to the United Kingdom when she was very young with her Indian parents. My father, David, or as his siblings would call him 'Agyei' is of Ghanian descent and moved to the United Kingdom at the age of 10 years old. My parents met in college and had faced a fair share of struggle from their parents because of their relationship. It wasn't long before my mother was kicked out of her house for being with a Black man, and it wasn't too long after that, that my parents created four children, myself being the second child. At first glance, when looking at me I look Black with a hint of something else, however it wouldn't be until you ask me where I am from that you will discover the depths of my Indian heritage. My mother very resilient, has always been open about her past and has been able to transcend light on situations that I might be going through. Recently, I sat down with my mother and we discussed some of the past events that happened in primary school where racism was very evident from teachers.

Event 1

This conversation with my mother was in relation to an event which took place in Year 1, where I, as a child at the age of 5 made a major mistake of stealing money from my teacher. This event which took place, was not merely because I felt to steal, but it stemmed from being in a school where the White students' parents were able to afford scooters, new trainers, sweets after school and the latest toys. Hearing your parents disagree about being unable to afford things placed me in a situation where I believed I was helping as opposed to doing something terrible. Myself and another child, Jamar, who came from a similar socioeconomic background, but where his mother has 5 different children to four different dads, took an opportunity (one, which in my adult life I admit was wrong) to try and aid the financial problems at home. Speaking with my mum about this event, she recalls some words that the headteacher, a White woman, had to say about my actions:

Neina: *Miss Madison was very strict, and she always picked on the Black children. I know when you stole that money it was because you were either getting involved with the wrong children or it was because you knew that we were struggling. When Miss Madison called us into the school to tell us what you done, I remember her shouting at you and saying, "this is a disgrace, you have no potential." It was at this stage that I had to stop her and tell her that what she was saying was* *wrong and no matter what has happened she should not be telling you, a five year old, that you have "no potential". If this had been a White child, I doubt she would have told that child that they have "no potential".*

This was clearly racism and she was not merely just an angry teacher disciplining a child. I have learnt on my educational journey, that there are many teachers who are racist and many teachers who treat Black and White children differently. It was only recently that I found out that my mother had no clue that I was removed from lessons for an extended period of time without her knowing due to this incident. Being "removed from class: a form of exclusion from equal access to schooling but not a form of exclusion that shows up in official data," (Gillborn, D. 2008. p.61) was a tactic used to ensure they could enforce punishment without my parents knowing.

Event 2

I specifically remember being taught by Miss Karen in Year 3 and remember having such a difficult time in school throughout that academic year. Miss Karen was a White woman from South Africa and she had come to teach in my primary school class which was predominantly White, with a few Black students and one Asian student.

Neina: *I remember when you were in Year 3, there was a fight between two White boys in the playground at lunch time. You went to try and stop the fight and instead of Miss Karen your Year 3 teacher penalising the two White boys who were fighting, she attempted to penalise you. She said that you were not allowed to play football for a week, but she allowed the two White boys to play, even though they were the ones who were fighting. It's a shame that you were trying to do the right thing and stop the boys and she told you that you are not allowed to play. Once this happened, I told you not to get involved in stopping any fights.*

Church

As I got older, naturally my interests developed. Every Sunday, my parents would take myself, my sister and brothers to a small church in the deprived, high crime-driven area of Peckham which would later move to a similar area, Brixton. It was here that my love for rap grew profoundly. I attended a predominantly Black Pentecostal church, which was headed by a White male pastor. It was here that I made some friends, Steven and Godfrey. Myself, my older brother Joseph, Steven and Godfrey would leave the church service and rap outside or in the hallways of the church, seeing who had the best lyrics. It was not long after our bunking of the pastor's service that we decided to put together a Christian rap group called "The Free Boys[4]". The Free Boys may have started in a small church in Peckham, but it eventually branched out to be huge, as we would perform rap songs in other churches, competitions, church camps, Notting Hill Carnival and the national radio. As teenagers, music acted as a distraction for us and coming from backgrounds where we could easily have been involved in gang violence and crime, we stayed on track for a long period of time. It was not long after the buzz that we were receiving, that a DVD was released in the UK originally from America by (Lewis, C. 2009) called "*Ex Ministries – The Truth Behind Hip Hop*". This DVD was the demise of The Free Boys as the message of the DVD was taken out of proportion by the pastor of the church. The message of the DVD was in relation to rap music and hip-hop, exposing all of the secrets behind the music industry and ultimately saying that the genre of music was evil. It was after the release of this DVD and the viewing of it that the pastor, despite our positive message, decided that The Free Boys were no longer allowed to perform in the church due to rap being a "secular" genre of music. This decision ultimately caused the group to split up and it was not long after, that one of the members went to prison for a robbery. The importance

---

[4] The name of the rap group has been changed.

of us making music was significant, especially as we were all at risk of going down the wrong path before music came into play. Taking the music away, confirms that without it, the path can be very dangerous. I tell this story not to diminish the church in the slightest, and as a devout Christian, I believe that because rap is a racialised genre of music, when White people who are not embedded in the culture are mis-given information without their own proper research, it is problematic.

Secondary School

In 2003, I attended Robert Baron School[5] in South London. The school had recently been appointed a new Headteacher named Mr. Rudra in 2001 who was attempting to turn the school around for the better. Mr. Rudra originally from Goa (India) worked in a school which was predominantly full of Black and Hispanic students. My attendance of this school would later play a major part in the choice of school I would work in when becoming a qualified teacher. Students who attended Robert Baron School, a Catholic school, which had strict rules that many did not adhere to, came from different parts of South London. The school had its problems, and the school also had a culture of gangs, drugs and violence due to everyone's scattered locations. One of the rules which was enforced from the beginning of school in Year 7 was that students were not allowed to rap in the playground. This was due to the stigma which rap had created in the early 2000s and a lack of understanding about the depths of rap from the Headteacher and the Senior Leadership Team. Despite this being a rule, students, including myself would huddle around in a group and rap to someone beatboxing or to an instrumental backing track which was illegally downloaded onto a mobile phone. For the five years of schooling, this rule was enforced and for those five years, I would get into trouble for breaking this rule and would often sit in detention writing new lyrics.

---

[5] The name of the school has been changed.

School, Church, School

  I remember once, my mother was emptying my trouser pockets and was surprised to find lyrics which I had written on a piece of paper in detention:

> I'm sick of this school
> I swear down, it has stupid rules
> Mr. Rudra, Miss Molly they're all stupid fools
> Rap when I want, I'll keep breaking the rules
>
> They don't understand
> They'll remember when I have a mic in my hand
> Infront of a crowd going real ham
> Silly headteacher, why can't he just jam

This rap at the time, was one of many which I as a young adolescent felt free writing and one which I used to express myself as I felt oppressed being in a school that enforced such rules. Looking back at this situation, I realised that there was no reason for the school not to allow students to rap in small groups; it was no different to a group of girls doing each other's hair in the playground, or a group of boys celebrating when someone scored a goal during break time. Rap as a genre had created a stigma for itself of negativity, that those who were not understanding of this racialised genre did not take the opportunity to listen to or explore the many positive raps that were in the world. Although many of the students were rapping negative content, the raps which I was rapping in the playground was that of positive content which had transitioned from 'Christian Rap' to 'Conscious Rap', where I would talk about all of the problems within society and how we as a people needed to think about our actions.

  In Year 9, I was introduced to a new English teacher who would eventually take my class through to complete their GCSEs. Mr Clemshaw was not an immediately engaging teacher, however, he provided me with an opportunity in his class to create in a way that I envisioned creativity. He created a poetry lesson and set us homework whereby we had to write

School, Church, School

a poem about the events that were happening in the world with the use of newspaper clippings. These poems were later to be performed to the class. For my poem I decided that I would write a rap, which ultimately is a form of poetry. Mr Clemshaw was an elder White man and when asking me to perform my poem to the class, I said that I needed him to play a CD for me whilst I performed. Mr Clemshaw, without questioning me, put the CD into the CD player and played the instrumental backing track 'Hope' (Mitchell, C & Jordan, F. 2004).

> My mission today is to pray
> Why? cause we're in evil days
> There's even been tsunami waves
> Even hurricanes wars and earthquakes
> And politics (tics) having massive debates
>
> What ball game are you playing? Not the same as me
> People on the streets fighting and having envy
> Listen up, it's not the way to be
> Listen to this rap and listen up carefully
>
> Suicide bombers bombed the trains and the bus
> And the politics (tics) they always have a fuss
> And a young man's walking by who always has a cuss
> This don't apply to one person it applies to all of us
>
> There will be a day where we all live in harmony
> There will be a day where we all speak calmly
> There will be a day where we all live in peace
> And there will be a day where all the violence will cease

After I performed this rap, I received a standing ovation from the class, including Mr Clemshaw. Mr Clemshaw was able to see beyond the stigma of rap and was aware that rap was indeed poetry, of which he approved. Mr Clemshaw didn't only approve but he organised a joint assembly with the music teacher at the end of the school term and asked me to create a song to perform in front of the whole school, a song that included the rap which I had created in the class. This was ironic because rap as a genre was banned in my school, but it was given validation through a White male English teacher and the school turned a blind eye to this. All of the years that I was getting into trouble for rapping in the playground was ultimately voided through a piece of work that I produced in a structured schooling task. The content of the lyrics did not differ in any way and still followed the conscious message which I had been rapping in the school playground. This performance created a path and broke the stigma of rap within Robert Baron School as the music teacher would open up his classroom at break and lunch for students to go in, write lyrics and rap to CDs and although not a full 360 on the rules, there was some progress in rap becoming an accepted genre amongst White teachers.

4 School, Church, School Analysis

For the analysis of this section, it is important that I share three pieces of work written by students, alongside share three sections of conversations which were held with each individual student. The reason the analysis will be written this way is to explain the children's thought process and how this thought process is paralleled to mine as a child. This section covers three students' experiences, two of whom are in Year 10 and were asked to write a rap about the events that happen in Stave 1 of *A Christmas Carol* and one who is in Year 9 and was asked to write a rap about *A Raisin in the Sun* from the perspective of one of the characters.

School, Church, School Analysis

Brianna's work

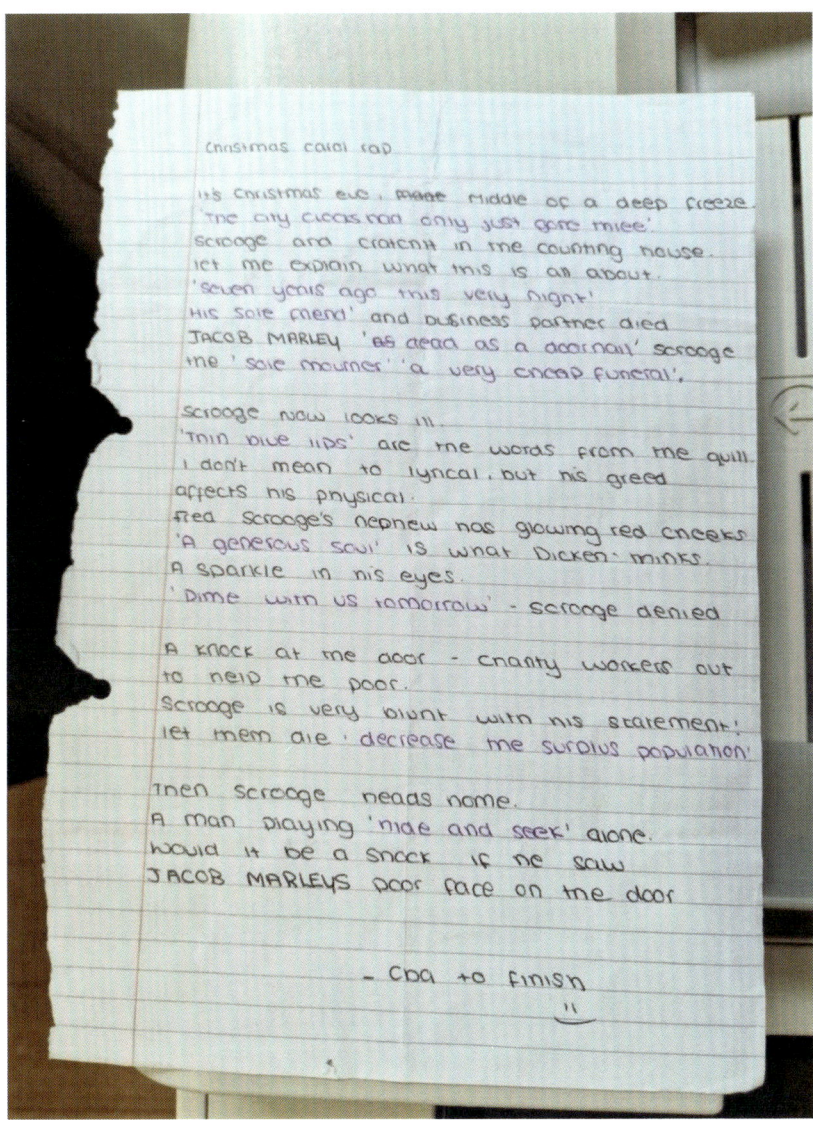

Brianna in many ways reminds me of myself in school. She is often disengaged and does not complete much of her work in class. Brianna was moved down to my class at the beginning of the 2021-2022 academic year and although a slow starter, is very capable and sporadically has bursts of brilliance like seen in this above rap. In this piece of work that Brianna created, but does not care to finish, as she writes "cba [can't be asked] to finish" it is clear that she puts effort into the task. This is evident as she took the time to include quotations such as "Seven years ago this very night", "dine with us tomorrow" and "thin blue lips" alongside write them in different colours so that I as a teacher could see that she had gone above and beyond. Tasks like this are beneficial for students such as Brianna, who are deemed as "problematic" and "disengaged" because these tasks are engaging. These tasks are not only engaging, but they are tasks that act as an aid to English as a curriculum through the interweaving of rap generating leeway for the curriculum to be accessible and inclusive.

It is clear to me that "many factors can and do influence a lesson and the learning that can happen in it" (Cantwell, 2014, p.24) and students like Brianna need to be engaged through lessons whereby they are able to understand the wider purpose and rationale in the tasks which ultimately builds confidence and a need to partake in meaningful activities. Had I asked Brianna to immediately write an essay about *A Christmas Carol*, she would have most likely not attempted the task. By taking the steps I did as a teacher through the use of music at first instance, acts as a deterrent to students later saying "I don't know" when giving them an essay and acts as a support mechanism to the students to feel confident in writing about a topic. Although the "reading and the thinking that takes place in the classroom [is] a collaborative process that involves teacher and student [this] cannot be isolated from the social, cultural and world experience of all of us," (Turvey, Brady, Carpenter & Yandell, 2006, pg.59) through the incorporation of something that Brianna was familiar with, this later allowed her to write paragraphs and essays in the classroom and do well in her initial test for *A Christmas Carol* as many of the quotations which were added in her rap was added into her essay.

Jahmelia's work

A christmas carol rap

Mr Scrooge? he was an old miser.
But little did we know that he would get wiser.
He met three spirits that changed his life.
Or he would've been doomed in the afterlife.
He didn't wanna end up like his bestie Marley
Cause he was chained up and looking gnarly.
Marley wore the chains he forged in life,
And so would Scrooges if he didn't get his priorities right.
Scrooges girl left cause he was acting kinda funny,
But deep down inside his love was stronger for his money.
The ghost of christmas past, with the appearance of 'a child',
Made scrooge reminisce, now his hate for love was wild.
Spirit number two was a great, big abundance
And now scrooges prestige behaviour was redundant.
The last ghost had a demonic demeanour,
Seeing scrooge so scared, was an absolute screamer.
The ghost approached, slowly and gravely,
One last move and scrooge would've turned to gravy.
It then showed scrooge his very near future,
But let's see if he changes, or was it all just a rumour?

Jahmelia is a student who is similar to Brianna, except, she is a student who overtly will decide not to do something and does not care about the consequences. Jahmelia clearly thought about this task, not only through lexical choice, but through rhythm, pace and the delivery of the rap. Jahmelia understood that a rap did not need to follow the generic English structure and slang words and colloquialisms were still valid in such a task. She includes powerful lines that don't follow the generic English syntactical rules such as:

"Scrooges girl left cause he was moving kinda funny,
But deep down inside his love was stronger for the money"

In a school such as David Lean Academy[6], whereby there is a disconnect between teacher and student experiences, it was evident from the start of joining that "[state] schools are not very interested in helping young people develop the sorts of [interpretive] practices [such as this] that I think are important. In schools, studying literature continues to mean reading a lot of it rather quickly and being able to identify literary devices and write critical essays" (Sumara, 2002, p.157). With emphasis in current government direction for "Standard English" (Gov.uk 2021) this is often operationalised uncritically, without a sophisticated understanding of the dialectal nature of English, alongside class, race and cultural issues around dialects, and had the Head of Department seen this, she may have deemed this unaligned with the teaching standards. Without an understanding of dialects and the power of language, the notion that "Standard English" (Gov.uk 2021) is in itself racist as it excludes that of non-white language forms. This said, education is moving in a direction, where lessons are more about 'knowledge' and less about 'interpretation' which is dangerous and means that students such as Jahmelia will be deemed as 'unsuccessful' because she

---

[6] The name of the school has been changed.

is able to respond extremely well and formulate ideas but has openly expressed that she does not care much about 'knowledge'. This task for Jahmelia, was perfect and one which fitted the demographic of the class entirely, as she was able to "draw from communal funds of knowledge," (Yosso, T. 2005. p.76) and not only write with clear rhythm but incorporate colloquial language. Jahmelia's work also deployed poetic devices drawn wittily from the original text as she would use quotations from the text such as "Marley wore the chains he forged in life" but without knowing, in this whole rap, Jahmelia would use alliteration, ambitious vocabulary, sibilance, tone, colloquial language and rhetorical questions, all of which I would later use in a lesson to explain what each of these linguistic devices were and the importance of 'ambitious vocabulary' in the tests that they would sit in the coming year. I would use "demonic demeanour" to explain alliteration, "abundance" to explain ambitious vocabulary, "seeing Scrooge so scared" to explain sibilance, "kinda funny" to explain colloquial language and "or was it all just a rumour?" to explain rhetorical question. This very notion that Jahmelia wrote a rap without the explicit knowing of linguistic devices is of a similar experience to mine whereby I wrote the rap about the world in Mr. Clemshaw's class. It did not cross my mind during the task that I would add in repetition, colloquialisms, plosives, alliteration, and the power of three. If teachers read students' raps in depth, through the use of annotating their students' work, they can discover all of the linguistic features that raps have to offer, which can ultimately provide follow up lessons delving deeper into these. Following a conversation with Jahmelia, it was clear that she understood the process of writing a rap, she was able to identify what was easy, what was difficult.

Me: Do you think that writing raps have benefits when revising? If so how, if not how?

Jahmelia: Yeah, I think they do, cause like you see everyone my age nowadays, they remember lyrics of songs, because it's catchy but they don't remember just the basic stuff in a book where it's just all laid out in front of you. Putting it in a rap is like, you add more rhythm, it helps you remember it.

Me: Did you write this with or without an instrumental?

Jahmelia: I did it in my head, there was a video on YouTube, and I listened to it and I went with the music in the background, but my words.

Me: What do you think the music did for you in terms of your writing? What would be the difference between you writing without the music and then you writing with the music? What's the difference?

Jahmelia: Without the music, it's actually hard, like it's difficult, cause you don't know how to start it off, you don't know how fast you want it to be, how slow you want it to be, but with the music, you kind of get an understanding how you want it to be laid out.

In doing this task, Jahmelia's experience was very similar to mine growing up. When I was in Mr Clemshaw's class, when presenting my rap to the class, I used an instrumental backing track. The sounds and melodies of the instrumental backing track is what allowed me to write with precise rhythm as the tempo would allow me to take out and include specific words. Teachers need to understand that pupils, although at times may be disengaged or misbehave, they have a lot to offer in the classroom that teachers can learn from and, "I critique the assumption that students of colour come to the classroom with cultural deficiencies" (Yosso, T. 2005. p.70). I further argue that students of colour at times come to the classroom with more cultural knowledge than teachers, especially in schools such as David Lean Academy where many of the teachers are not embedded within the community that they teach in. Students like Jahmelia are valuable to the education system as her "community cultural wealth [is important] to transform the process of schooling," (Yosso, T. 2005. p.70) as long as those in charge pay attention to all that could be learnt from students like Jahmelia. Jahmelia was able to identify ways in which she learnt and what made writing easier for her, as she acknowledged that writing without music was hard, so she put on a popular rap song from YouTube and wrote to the instrumental backing track. Jahmelia understands that pace and tempo is extremely important with rap and poetic form and in her piece of work she confesses that the instrumental backing track acted as an aid for her. This was significant as "manipulating the music of [her] oral compositions, and adding instrumental or body percussion [helped her] feel the significant rhythms and build on the linguistic flexibility." (Grainger, Goouch & Lambirth, 2005, p. 131). Rap music, although racialised as a genre is not to be diminished or excluded from the classroom, it is to be used to its widest abilities, especially in the 21st century where music is incorporated into nearly all elements of media and we as a people are surrounded by it constantly.

School, Church, School Analysis

Malik's work[7]

> Our whole family suffering and walter thinks its funny
> This one reason why I didnt tell him I have a baby in my tummy,
> I want to buy a house with the 10K cheque,
> Walter at the bar tryna place some bets,
> Our family poor I cant give no-one 50 cent,
> Travis said hes for greatness at thats what he meant,
> Walter hates when I mention we are poor,
> Thats why he gave Travis 1 dollar when he walk through the door,
> I andmire walter failing at as am man.
> Mama know so she sould give him a bank.
> Benatha dont believ in God so im failing as a mum.
> This is because im dumb,
> She wants to be a doctor so good for her,
> how can that be when our house im made out of fur,
> I feel sorry for walter, Tavis, Benettha and the baby,
> I wished walter never laid me,

Malik is in Year 9 and this rap was written as a homework task from the perspective of a chosen character – in this case, he chose Beneatha from the play *A Raisin in the Sun* (Hansberry, L. 1959). Malik is a very hard-working student who has overcome many educational hurdles. Initially when meeting Malik, I would classify him as a reluctant reader, I later came to find out, he was reluctant to read due to his dyslexia. For Malik, his dyslexia meant that he "often lack[ed] adequate fluency skills [and] stumble[d] over words [and made] frequent reading errors." (Texas Scottish Rite Hospital for Children, 2014) and (Pilgrim, J. 2015. P15) I did not

---

[7] A copy of the rap typed out can be found in the Appendix.

understand as a teacher how impactful a task like this would be for Malik as when I asked him to rap his lyrics to me, for the first time in my experience of witnessing him read, he did not stutter or fumble any of the words on his page. When reflecting into the reason as to why Malik did not stutter or fumble any words, I recognised that "poems for children are often short and they contain rhythm, rhyme, and meaning, making practice easy, fun, and rewarding" (Eunice Kennedy Shriver National Institute of Child Health and Human Development, 2001, p. 24) and (Pilgrim, J. 2015. P18). When speaking with Malik, I came to recognise the importance of music in the classroom, especially in unification with students who come from Black families, because for Malik this played a significant part in his upbringing.

Me: I set this as a homework task about *A Raisin in the Sun* for you to do alone by yourself. How did it feel doing this task alone by yourself?

Malik: It felt quite easy, cause, the way my family grew up, we all grew up listening to music, so it just came to me.

Me: If you just turn the page for me, you didn't do a plan. Why didn't you do a plan?

Malik: When I started doing it, there wasn't a real plan for me to follow, it was not stage by stage, it was just write it down, I would have felt limited and this allows me to be creative with my words.

Me: Why do you think that your perspective is important?

Malik: Our perspective is important because people get to see the world how we believe it is. They see it how we see it and how we interpret it.

Me: Do you think many teachers see the world how you see it?

Malik: No

I concluded that Malik was similar to a musician in the sense that "rarely would a musician perform music without practicing it on multiple occasions." (Pilgrim, J. 2015. P18) and he most likely took the opportunity to practice his lyrics multiple times. I resonated with this, as similarly to when I was in Mr. Clemshaw's class, I wrote my lyrics without the limitations of a plan, but I practiced multiple times before performing to the entire class; and thus redrafted, corrected and tweaked parts to make it perfect. This task allowed me as a teacher to gain a deeper understanding and separated me as a teacher as many "teachers [lacked the] knowledge needed to teach struggling readers, particularly children with dyslexia (Washburn, Joshi, & Binks-Cantrell, 2011) and (Pilgrim, J. 2015. P15). This task formed an open relationship between myself and Malik as I understood early in the year his needs and how he is able to overcome some of his reading difficulties and as "dyslexia is a visual-processing deficit rather than a language-processing deficit," (Dyslexia Help, 2015) and (Pilgrim, J. 2015. P15) I was able to set Malik separate tasks which involved creating raps to better his reading skills.

The very fact that Malik grew up listening to music, means that he was able to include his cultural capital to aid his "visual-processing deficit" (Pilgrim, J. 2015. P15) and although the standard practice at David Lean Academy might suggest that the task had not 'challenged' Malik as he found the task "easy" this is not the case as this acted as a long term aid for his dyslexia and as "music links the functions of the right and left hemispheres of the brain so that they work together to make learning quick and efficient," (Davies, 2000) and (Pilgrim, J. 2015. P17) the more this task is offered and completed by students like Malik, the better position students are in to learn quickly how to break barriers and learning stigmas.

Although I myself did not grow up with dyslexia, in my teaching practice, I have come across multiple students with the condition, and have seen the impact it has on students' perspective of themselves. Dyslexia often makes students shy, anxious and at times feel inadequate, however "there are many similarities between literacy acquisition and musical development, and teaching that combines language arts instruction with music can be most effective." Davies (2000) and (Pilgrim, J. 2015. P17) and for Malik, it is particularly important that he "[found] a teacher who understands dyslexia" (British Dyslexia Association 2022). The conjunction of these strategies have deemed effective for students such as Malik and when used with "evidence-based strategies for improving fluency, music has the potential to motivate student learning and may be a helpful way to practice fluency" (Register, 2001) and (Pilgrim, J. 2015. P17). Malik didn't only find the writing of the lyrics easy, he also mentioned that his "perspective is important because people get to see the world how [he] believe[s]it is" and that "They see it how we see it and how we interpret it." This is extremely important that Malik understands from such a young age the significance of his perspective as a young Black boy; and although he does not believe that many teachers see the world how he sees it, this difference in viewpoint is something that Malik if he does not already know will find out about when he gets older and transitions to work with different people from different backgrounds. This experience acted for Malik, became an intersection between pupil voice, philosophies of knowledge and an insight into race, all of which it became evident to me that Malik had a deep understanding of.

5 Rap Therapy and NQT Teaching

I completed university in 2013 with no real vision as to what I would do next. By this stage, I had taken a break from music as I felt that there was no real market for the conscious music which I was making. My mother always told me to go into teaching, however I had no interest in working with children and didn't feel I had the discipline for such a career path. I bounced from job to job and worked in different fields and in 2016 I landed a job as a Bus Driver. As a Bus Driver, I would work long and gruelling hours with an inconsistent sleep pattern; however, it was during my bus driving days that I was able to rekindle my love for music. As a Bus Driver, it is very difficult to keep focus throughout the journeys, so to keep me awake and focused, I would put a headphone in my right ear and cover it with a hat and listen to music throughout the journeys, my one rule being, not to touch my phone or change the music throughout the journey. As I was driving the route 64 on a cold winter's day, an instrumental backing track from my playlist started to play in my headphones and automatically, I began to create a rap as I was driving. This small encounter with this instrumental backing track led me to later bringing a paper pad and pen on the bus whilst I drove my route. I would put an instrumental backing track on repeat and periodically stop at bus stops and press the button that says, "the driver has been instructed to wait at this bus stop for a short time to help even out the service," to write out the lyrics that were in my head. On occasions, I would have longer break times at work, some lasting up to four hours and within this time, I would rush home, record some lyrics or organise for a videographer to come and shoot a music video. In 2017 I ended up releasing an Extended Project (EP) called 'Invisible Guidelines' which highlighted all of the problems within my area and took listeners on an honest journey of the problems within the neighbourhood. 'Invisible Guidelines' was recognised by *The Metro, The Guardian, Local Media* and many more news outlets. Oddly enough, I wasn't interested in the fame and despised it quite a bit. During one of my breaks as a Bus Driver, I sat with my brother Joseph in the coffee shop, and we discussed the prospects of me starting a business. My one condition with this business was that it had to be music related. Eventually, I created an idea and it was agreed between Joseph and me that I would start a company called 'Rap Therapy' whereby I would go into different schools and deliver workshops to students teaching them about the importance of rap and aiding with their mental health blending music and English. Initially when introducing Rap Therapy to multiple schools, the programme was turned down due to its name. Merging two words which had negative stigmas attached to them deemed difficult and there were four occasions, where White male teachers would suggest that we as a company should change the name, this didn't take place. This suggestion demonstrated that they did not understand what we were doing and its importance. Throughout this journey, the first opportunity occurred when a Black female teacher at a school in Croydon allowed me to run Rap Therapy in the school. This Black female teacher opened up plenty of doors for Rap Therapy and introduced us to many schools within the borough, which eventually spread further into different boroughs and across London and Surrey. I often wonder how long it would have taken Rap Therapy to get into schools in a heavily White dominated system without the aid of this Black woman.

    As Rap Therapy began to grow, I was able to employ staff to go into schools to represent the company and deliver impactful workshops. It was during this growth period that I decided to take my mother's advice and embark on a Secondary PGCE course. After the completion of my PGCE, when choosing a secondary school to work in, I wanted it to be of similar type to the school which I grew up in - Robert Baron School. The school which I ended up working in, was in a centralised part of South London, whereby, gang culture and misguidance was the epitome of many of these students' lives. As a Newly Qualified Teacher (NQT), I came into teaching with amazing and ambitious ideas and aspired to use rap within my classroom to teach English. I understood the power of rap in education, not only because I rapped or had seen the impact of Rap Therapy, but because when I was in school, I would take notes that I was given by teachers, and I would turn these into memorable raps which helped me pass my GCSEs. Knowing this, I wanted to pass this knowledge down to the younger generation, but as a teacher, I also wanted to provide students with the opportunity to create and express their own interpretation on different topics and ideas. As my teaching days progressed, I would tell teachers about Rap Therapy, however the only teachers who seemed to show a keen interest or understood the impact that this business would have, were teachers from Black or ethnic minority backgrounds. As the only Black person within a White department of six core English teachers, when explaining Rap Therapy to teachers within the department, often it was brushed off or was given a patronising smile. At this stage, I thought that it was just awkwardness due to not understanding such a business model, however I came to later realise through other experiences (which are described in greater detail later in this research) that this was due to the naïve understanding of what this racialised genre - rap - represented as to why these White teachers didn't pay the business and impact any attention; as rap played no role in their life or their culture.

  As an English teacher, I was able to build great relationships with children and kept an open and honest relationship which worked both ways. This relationship, I would later find out was extremely important not only for me as an English teacher, but for the students as I would later receive multiple cards in my departure from the school which had comments in cards such as "I see you as a father figure" and "You are like an uncle to me." The relationship and culture in my classroom was different to all of the other English teachers, as we were open enough to have conversations that went slightly off topic and conversations that covered the important elements of life outside of the school walls. My relationship with children didn't only cause slight jealousy amongst the White English teachers who found it difficult to build these bonds, but it was acknowledged by the local council as they contacted me to deliver a pre-recorded speech online, with the plans to circulate this to every school in South London. The local council asked me to create a speech, explaining to students across the borough where I came from and what I have achieved musically and in my business. I spoke heavily about my past encounter where I stole money from my Year 1 teacher and delved deeper into the word 'potential' and what it means. Upon completion, the local council were happy with the speech and circulated it to schools across the borough.

    I sent the video which I created to the headteacher via email which read:

Hi Charles,

I hope you are well and my apologies for the weekend email. I just wanted to let you know that a few years ago I did a speech for a group of schools in South London through the council's 'Shoot High' campaign. This speech was extremely successful, and the students were really engaged, and I was asked to give another speech this year. Due to the covid-19 circumstances this speech had to be delivered as a pre-recorded online video. The speeches aim to inspire pupils in South London and encourage them to pursue successful career paths. The aim is to reach predominantly Black and ethnic minority groups; however, the wider audience is all students.

I was thinking that this might be a really good video to circulate to form tutors to show during tutor time at some point over the next couple of weeks. The video is going to be circulated to other schools South London also (not through me through the council) and I think the message could possibly reach and inspire students, especially those who are disengaged to think about their choices more carefully. As this was online, there are videos embedded into the speech alongside pictures. Please see the link to the video: https://www.youtube.com/watch?v=-2ILt4b8eSo&ab_channel=The Local Council[8]

Kind regards,
Bhishma

This email which I had written, did not receive a reply. Initially, I thought that he might not have seen the email, however I later found out from a Black colleague of mine and childhood friend, Johnathan, who was the Head of Key Stage 3 at the time, that the Headteacher *had* seen the video. The Headteacher approached Johnathan who ironically was dealing with an incident where two boys had been selling sweets in school and said, "Bhishma sent me a speech, he was quite a bad boy in school it seems, he used to sell sweets". When Johnathan informed me of this, I felt that the Headteacher had deliberately misinterpreted the message which was being told throughout the whole speech. He also misunderstood the reasoning as to why, I, an underprivileged Black boy, who came from a family who did not have much was selling sweets in school. In a predominantly Black school, which was headed by a White male headteacher who had been Oxford educated and disconnected from the area which he led the school, it was

---

[8] The link to the video has been changed.

naïve of me to believe that he would understand the importance of this speech.

Although this speech was not acknowledged by the Headteacher, the local council acknowledged it and later decided that they would like me to be the 'Racial Justice Champion' for my school. This position was pro bono and allowed me to attend periodic meetings with different schools in order to provide the same opportunities and make a difference for Black and ethnic minority students within the school. When the local council had appointed me this position, I informed the Headteacher of this position and I was ignored. I then sent a follow up email as the local council were also ignored when they attempted to contact him as he did not see the immediate importance for such a role.

Hi Charles,

I hope you are doing well.

I know it is quite a busy time for David Lean Academy, but I was wondering if you saw my previous email about the video that I did through the local council's Shoot High campaign?

If you have seen the video, it would be great to know if David Lean Academy be planning to do anything with this video e.g. show the students the video during tutor time? I think there is a clear message in the video about 'potential' and Aim High have commended it for being one of the best videos they have seen.

In addition to the above, I wanted to find out if you have responded to Laura from the council in regard to the Racial Justice *Champion position? I attended a meeting on behalf of David Lean Academy today and I think this is not only an important role, but a role that benefits the school as a community if all staff knew this is how I am helping David Lean Academy on a wider scale. I think if there is time during the briefing on Thursday, mentioning it to staff would be a great idea and very beneficial, because we can then all make a collective effort to ensure Black and ethnic minority students get the best opportunities now which will help them in the near future.*

Kind regards,
Bhishma

This also did not receive a reply. Nor was it mentioned again (though the activities of other staff were regularly announced at morning briefing). Ironically, when stepping down from this position, it was re-allocated to a teacher of his choice - a White teacher within the school and they were praised in briefing for their efforts and for stepping up and taking the position; there was still no acknowledgment for my efforts and work. The racism within this whole experience was quite evident to me and I wondered why it wasn't communicated to staff or children when I was the 'Racial Justice Champion', but it was communicated to everyone when another White male teacher took over the position.

    The relationships in my classroom were robust not only through open communication but also through a pedagogic approach that included techniques such as the incorporation of rap into lessons. Although I was instructed to "stay on the Scheme of Work" by the Head of Department, Carly, (a White middle-class woman), I still incorporated rap and linked it to the Scheme of Work. The students who found topics and themes difficult were able to create interpretations and were able to convert these older canonical stories which were being read into modern day raps. This method which was consolidated in the lessons was not only a fun experience for the children, but it taught revision methods, interpretation and cleared up any misconceptions about the stories at hand. This broke the stereotype of rap for many students, as they were unaware that they were able to turn school texts into raps which they will remember for life.

6 Rap Therapy and NQT Teaching Analysis

When reflecting on all of the events that took place as an NQT at David Lean Academy, I now conclude that I was subject to a substantial amount of racism. This at times was conscious and overt and at times was due to a lack of education and insight to culture, socioeconomic backgrounds and race as a whole. I think back to the reasoning as to why I picked David Lean Academy to teach in, when there were multiple schools I could have entered to teach as an NQT, one of which was a well-known Grammar School. My reasoning for picking David Lean Academy was because I felt a close connection to the students and the community which it resided in. A deprived background, where many of the children were Pupil Premium, a background that reminded me of my school days. A school like David Lean Academy needed more Black teachers as the school system and "curriculum [is] a culturally specific artifact designed to maintain a White supremacist master script[s]" (Ladson-Billings, G, 1998, p.18) and in a school whereby those who are teaching Black children, are predominantly middle class White women, teaching arguably White racist men's canonical texts, there needs to be more representation and perspective within the classroom, hence why this school was chosen. One might argue that no matter the school which I embarked upon my career, I would be teaching the same canon, however, the key difference between teaching children of colour and that of those who are from middle class White backgrounds is the way in which texts can be interpreted through experience. This is not to say there is no need for me to teach in a middle classed comprehensive school, where the majority of students are White, but teaching in these different schooling demographics serve different purposes:

1. Teaching in a predominantly Black school, allows me as an English practitioner to not only highlight problems within the canon but permits me to have an active voice as to what Black children are reading. I will delve deeper into this, when I speak on "The Globe Theatre Trip".
2. To teach in a predominantly White school, this would allow me as an English practitioner to not only share my experiences but to explain to White children the problems, which ultimately would be a completely different angle to how I explain this to Black children; this also requires a high amount of discipline as an English teacher.

Overall, there is a lack of Black teachers, particularly male teachers teaching English within the United Kingdom and the less Black teachers there are speaking against particular authors and their racist undertones, the longer the curriculum will stay the same.

When thinking about the interactions I had with teachers, explaining to them what Rap Therapy is and its impact, I came to realise that the majority of the teachers with whom I was in contact with didn't understand the benefits based on their disconnect and very different upbringings to the students at hand. Not only did I understand that "if we offer children the chance to play with the tunes of their popular culture and oral transitions, they learn to experiment with these rhythms in their own voices and discover new cadences and melodies to savour and remember," (Grainger, Goouch & Lambirth, 2005, p. 131) I also understood and reflected that I as a child used methods in order to remember schoolwork, something that I wanted students in my classroom to adopt, which they ultimately did. Through "[transgressing] the traditional view of the teacher's role" (Britton, 1987, p. 25), I was able to use "Hip-hop [and rap] [as a] counter-narrative to the authority of the official school curriculum and [used it as a] medium to engage [students]" (Shelby-Caffey, 2018, p.72).

Education has developed and has become less about teaching being merely about children, it has developed to become more about careers, politics and getting to the top of the career ladder. David Lean Academy had multiple young members of the Senior Leadership Team (SLT) who were once teachers who progressed perhaps too quickly, and this becomes problematic because there is a risk that when career progression for managers dominates, children cease to be at the heart of education for teacher leaders. Although "race is always already present in every social configuring [of] our lives" (Ladson-Billings, G, 1998, p.9) it was powerfully evident in David Lean Academy. Not only was I the only Black English teacher, but there was no diversity amongst SLT in a school that has predominantly Black children and if I am to have a "critical perspective on the nature of politics and society in general," (Gillborn, D. 2008. p.28) it is clear that the school leadership is not a reflection of the children and the area as "society has been widely misrepresented and misunderstood," (Gillborn, D. 2008. p.28) as there are no Black members of SLT or governance that governs the schools newly merged partnership with a multi-trust academy - Knights Academy[9]. This is problematic, because if students don't see representations of themselves in leadership, they ultimately believe that the power lies with those of White skin tones and "racism requires sweeping changes," (Ladson-Billings, G, 1998, p.12) changes that don't only apply to the curriculum and input from teachers of ethnic origin, but changes that apply to leadership and who is at the top leading the school.

---

[9] The name of the trust has been changed.

As a teacher in the school, I have heard multiple White male teachers say that I am "good with Black boys because you are Black," whereas this might have some small elements of truth in it, this has racial undertones and diminishes the relationships I build with children which had ultimately nothing to do with race but more with creating safe spaces and building robust relationships. When leaving David Lean Academy, comments such as "I see you as a father figure" and "you are like an uncle to me" revealed to me that my classes were inclusive of all, and I provided a safe environment. The elements of a safe environment also stems from aspects of masculinity, many of which plenty of students do not have in their households. Comments such as "you're good with Black boys because you are Black," not only revealed jealousy but many White people think of "race strictly as an ideological concept" (Ladson-Billings, G, 1998, p.9). The mere thought that this might be the *only* reason as to why I am good with Black boys is not a fair or just statement to make.

When sending the email to Charles, not only did I feel disappointed that I did not receive a reply, but I felt undermined and was made to feel that I lacked integrity when he later approached Johnathan to discuss me in a way that Jonathan found to be dismissive. Little did Charles know that "the exchange of stories from teller to listener can help overcome ethnocentrism and the [unconscious] drive or need to view the world in one way" (Ladson-Billings, G, 1998, p.13). Instead of the headteacher taking the opportunity to learn about my decisions, he made a conscious choice to degrade my story through misinterpretation and further this through not presenting this to children who would have heavily benefited from it. Students in David Lean Academy were and still are going through similar situations that I went through as a child; this would have acted as an inspiration and could have deterred future suspensions, exclusions and in the future could have prevented students going down the wrong path, ultimately ending them dead or in jail. In order to understand children from particular demographics, it is important that teachers who do not reside or are not raised in these areas take every opportunity to learn from those who have grown up in similar socioeconomic backgrounds and this cannot happen if the "dialogue of people of colour has been silenced" (Ladson-Billings, G, 1998, p.14).

7 Learning during Lockdown

Prior to the lockdown, I was grateful to be given a Year 10 class who were labelled as 'mid-low' ability. Initially, when introducing myself to the class for the first time and setting them a few tasks to see how they wrote, I was surprised that a few of them were placed in this 'mid-low' prior attainment group. I believed that some of these students should have been placed in 'high ability' classes and they were unjustly placed into this class. Prior to the pivot to online learning during the first lockdown, I had spoken to the Head of Department to urge her to move the students up to a top set, as their being in a lower attainment class through selective grouping, would not push them if they were surrounded by students who are not thinking at a 'top set' level. This request, which was made at least 5 times was rejected by the Head of Department. The student in particular who stood out to me is a girl called Sabiti. Sabiti is a Black girl from Uganda, her first language is Luganda, however from speaking with her, unless you asked, you wouldn't have any idea that she spoke a second language. Sabiti has the highest work ethic within the class, perfecting her handwriting and thinking deeply about what she is being taught, asking for past papers and this was truly reflected throughout every piece of work which she carefully crafted. Sabiti from a young age clearly understood and was not oblivious to the fact that she did not come from a 'wealthy' background, and she understood that she needed to work hard to change this. Sabiti's depth of understanding about societal problems and the racial injustices around the world was evident and second to none in the class. Although very persistent and hardworking, she was a very loved student amongst her peers as she had the fine balance of knowing how to work hard but also knowing how to be social amongst others, which nurtured their adoration for her.

There are two pieces of work Sabiti created that are relevant to this study; the first being a rap about *A Christmas Carol* and the second being an analysis of (Morrison, M & Simmons, E 2002) *'Innocent Man'* rap in comparison to (Shakur, T & Jones, N. 2002) *'Thugz Mansion'* rap.

Ebenezer Scrooge thinks he's a winner
but he's a clutching, covetous old sinner
his appearance is cold, hard, sharp & thin
no one ever really wanted to chat to him

Ebenezer scrooge clerk is bob cratchit
my guy was so called he wasn't given a matchstick
bob cratchit was a humble soul
he had fire burning from a single coal

scrooge has a nephew his name is fred
he's a handsome young man with blonde hair on his head
fred said merry christmas when he came to visit
that's how you know he has christmas spirit

two gentlemen asked for money for the poor
scrooge wasn't gonna give him the money for sure
scrooge said no and he refused
didn't want to spend money so he made an excuse

scrooge was chilling on his own minding his buisness
then the ghost of jacob marley was what he witnessed
tried to get on his knees and beg for forgiveness
scrooge was so shocked his body was in stiffness

This piece of work, which was created by Sabiti, focuses on Stave 1 in *A Christmas Carol*. This was the first rap that Sabiti ever wrote and throughout this process, she ensured that she highlighted the qualities of Scrooge and the depths of his miserly ways. For someone who had just been taught Stave 1, it was clear that she was attentive to the details throughout the Stave as she highlights specific events such as "no one really wanted to chat to him" and "two gentlemen asked for money for the poor." Sabiti was able to retell the story of Stave 1 through her recollection of events in a format that she was new to but felt comfortable in. Sabiti also uses the ability to use quotations from the text such as "clutching, covetous old sinner" and although this was not a directive of the task, Sabiti took the initiative to include these quotes to directly present her understanding of the text and the relevance of the quotations used. Using quotations throughout her rap would later act as a pillar for Sabiti as she would later disclose to me that this rap helped her remember elements of the novella in her GCSE exam.

A second piece of work which is also relevant to this study is an incomplete piece of work which Sabiti created, whereby Sabiti's task was to read two separate raps created by DMX and Tupac and write about the similarities and differences between both artists' viewpoints and attitudes towards injustice within society.

> Both poets present there attitudes on injustice within society. Firstly, In the poem 'Innocent Man', DMX states himself as a 'victim of the 'dirt' that they are trying to throw on [his] name' which expresses how society attempts to portray the poet as wrongful. Likewise, Shakur in the poem 'Thugz Mansion' illustrates that 'no one knows [my] struggle' and recognises that light is only shed on 'the trouble'. He remarks that no one truly knows his inner feelings but only the 'trouble' reported by the media. Both poets feel choked by the negativity surrounding much of their persona.
>
> Now, there are noticeable differences in both poem through the structure of the poem. In 'Thugz Mansion', in the first stanza, he uses an AAAA rhyme scheme however not throughout the poem; creating an irregular structure. The fact that there is no clear structure presents a representation of his life. Whereas, in 'Innocent Man', the poet follows an AABB structure.
>
> Overall, both poets express how unfairly they were treated within society and had no support system.

In the first paragraph, Sabiti not only uses effective discourse markers such as "firstly" and "likewise", but she is able to decipher the lyrics and zoom into specific words such as "victim" and "dirt" which reflect the injustice that both rappers talk about in their lyrics. Sabiti is able to not only understand the poems, but she is able to understand the thoughts and feelings of each rapper throughout the start of the poem to the end and make links to society judging them as each of them feel "choked by the negativity surrounding much of their persona". In paragraph two, it is clear that Sabiti has an understanding of poetic devices and structure as she mentions "irregular structure" and "rhyme scheme" and is able to compare the two poems and their rhyme schemes. Sabiti, only having a total of 12 minutes to write this comparison is reflective of her ability to work to a high standard in short spaces of time.

During the pandemic, the whole of the Year 10 cohort had to complete their January assessments. These assessments were under new conditions as there was no contact with students and teachers, meaning that the assessments needed to be completed online via Google Docs. The question which students were to answer was the following:

| 0 | 8 |

Starting with this extract, explore how Dickens uses the Cratchit family to show the struggles of the poor.

Write about:

- how Dickens uses the Cratchit family to show the struggles of the poor in this extract
- how Dickens uses the Cratchit family to show the struggles of the poor in the novel as a whole.

[30 marks]

With this being the assessment question, I as a teacher was pleased as this Cratchit family and being poor was heavily covered before the revealing of the assessment question, meaning that my students were destined to do well. After this assessment was completed, I as a classroom teacher was to mark my classes' work and then it was to be moderated by the

Head of Department. During the moderation process, there was a discrepancy with a few students' marks, the marks that were requested to be brought down were all students who were Black, Sabiti being one of the students. The Head of Department accused these students of cheating on their tests. It was said by the Head of Department that these students used the internet to answer the question, however this could not have been the case as there was no copying or paraphrasing from any of the sources that were available on the internet at the time nor did any of the accused students' work look similar to one another. To add salt to the wound, throughout the duration of the year, there had only been two White girls in my class, one of whom did not do the test, however the one who did complete the test, the Head of Department asked me to raise her grade by 4 points, bringing her to a higher-grade boundary. This was unjust because the quality of work was not of the calibre where it needed to be raised.

Disputing the notion that the students had cheated, as a means to resolve this, the Head of Department asked me to have an initial conversation with the students to ask them openly if they had cheated on their test. All of the students denied the cheating, but Sabiti's work was still penalised, and her grade was dropped unreasonably. Through this event, I had a conversation online with Sabiti about the cheating allegation and it was there that Sabiti explained to me that "being Black at times can be stressful as [she] did not cheat." Sabiti being an honest student, would have openly told me if she had cheated, but the very fact that she understood that her race in this instance played a massive part in the accusation was upsetting for her as she had worked hard but also for me as a Black teacher. I explained to her that I resonated with her and that I believed every word she said. I told her that being Black in this world at times can be difficult, but it doesn't mean that she cannot be great. I explained to her that she has a voice, and it is very important that it is not silenced. After this conversation, to prove to the Head of Department that I had the conversation with Sabiti, I sent her a message asking her to confirm that she had not cheated.

 3 Feb 2021

Hi ▮▮▮▮ tried to call home to talk to you yesterday about your essay but could not get through!

Following the conversation we had today can you confirm that there was nothing copied off of the internet? L me know as soon as you can.

▮▮▮▮ 3 Feb 2021

Hey Mr. Asare. I wanted to give my input on what you said earlier and I totally agree with everything that you stated. People of colour are always expected to do the bare minimum but when we raise the bar its questiona and our intelligence is under minded simply because of the colour of our skin. But I don't tolerate it and I know my worth and I am more and capable of doing anything. This really pushes me to work hard and put 110% eff into and everything that I do. This is me technically ranting but also voicing my opinion and how I feel. I appreciate your teaching and every measure you put forward literally just so that we could get the best education and good grades. Your an excellent teacher. Have a nice rest of your day.
Thank you

This message from Sabiti was very relevant and she had every right to be upset about the situation. The very fact that this situation pushed Sabiti to "work hard and put 110% effort into everything" was inspiring as a teacher. Sabiti mentioning that "I appreciate your teaching and every measure you put forward literally just so that we could get the best education and good grades," reflectively made it hard not to see the criticism of Sabiti's performance as an implied attack on my professionalism, and - in the context of the clear inequity of behaviour regarding moderation - our shared racialised identities. The fact that a clear inference from the Head of Department's behaviour was that my teaching was not good enough for Sabiti to get these grades, the quicker I realised that Sabiti was better fitted in my class than her moving up to the Head of Departments class; it was at this stage, I stopped telling the Head of Department about the Black children who were doing well in my class in aims that they stay in my class so no further injustices were served.

When Sabiti reached Year 11, she later developed further to become an even more focused English student, whereby her opinion was very evident in her work and in her mock exams, she was able to attain a grade 5, a few marks off of a grade 6, meaning that she was working to a low B grade standard. With three weeks left to the exam, the Head of Department took 6 of the highest attaining pupils out of my class for scoring high in their mock exams and "strategically" moved these students into her class, alongside her White male friend's class. Her reasoning was so that she could move them from their current grade up a grade or two before the real GCSE exam – a claim difficult to credit because it was made with only some three weeks left before the exams. In those weeks that these students were moved to her and my colleague's class, the students would try and sneak into my class and would constantly complain about being moved at such a crucial time for them. Sadly, it seems more likely that the real reason for these moves was not for the benefit of the children, but to assist in massaging performance measures against appraisal targets. If these students later go on to do well in their final GCSE grades, these Black children will help these White teachers hit their appraisal targets, meaning that they are able to get a pay raise for the following year.

8 Learning during Lockdown Analysis

Sabiti is one of many students across the nation who are treated unfairly. Throughout this whole experience, Sabiti acted maturely and also had an advanced level of awareness about racism within society for her age. Through the message Sabiti sent me, whereby she is expressing the issues of being a Black student who is doing well, she and I were able to resonate with each other because "those injured by racism and other forms of oppression discover that they are not alone and moreover are part of a legacy of resistance to racism and the layers of racialized oppression" (Yosso, T. 2005. p.75). This experience is something that Sabiti was going through in 2020 and I as a young boy had gone through similar experiences when I was also a child going through the United Kingdom's education system. This problematic event caused both Sabiti and me to understand that we were not alone, and we were together in this oppressive act by the Head of Department. She was experiencing racism as a child in the education system and I as an adult in the education system, both of our experiences coming from the same person. This is detrimental to Black students, as when they get older, they will have resentment towards the system as opposed to want to aid and enhance the system. "DuBois (1903,1989) predicted that racism would continue to emerge as one of the United States' key social problems" (Yosso, T. 2005. p.70) and although he specifically speaks about the United States, this has been the case for the United Kingdom. With not many pieces of academic writing on race being produced by United Kingdom authors, I discovered that many of the theories and information about the American education system reverberated closely with that of the United Kingdom's education system, especially when considering race.

As a student, Sabiti writes uniquely and carefully thinks about what she writes beforehand. Giving Sabiti the task whereby she had to turn *A Christmas Carol* into a rap, allowed her as a student to "reflect upon meanings and by doing so acquired a new level of control, a critical awareness of her thought process" (Britton, 1987, p. 23). Sabiti was put in a position whereby even though she had never written a rap, through a pedagogic approach, she outperformed her expectations as she was able to find comfort in this new form of learning and present her own interpretations throughout the rap which she created. She was able to "[use her] own knowledge and [transform *A Christmas Carol*] [into her] own words." (Cantwell, 2014, p.25) Sabiti's ability to do such a task to such a high standard proved that she initially should not have been placed in a 'mid-low' prior attainment class.

Sabiti is the epitome of how education can not only ruin young people's experiences and perspectives of the system, but also how education can be contradictory. Even though Sabiti was consistently doing well in my class and was always scoring high, she was constantly rejected to move up to a higher set. "The contradictory nature of education, wherein schools most often oppress and marginalize while they maintain the potential to emancipate and empower," (Yosso, T. 2005. p.74) The Head of Department had the opportunity to move Sabiti alongside other up in the class, but the decision was made extremely late in the year, which has me questioning if this was to benefit the students or if there was an ulterior motive behind the class move. Education in this instance was less about the student and became more about the teachers, their comfortability, job progression and their income.

Sabiti, like many Black students within my school was not "born into a family whose knowledge is already deemed valuable" (Yosso, T. 2005. p.70) and does not come from a wealthy background. The Head of Department only felt necessary to move her up a set when she believed that she could, "access the knowledges of the middle and upper class and the potential for social mobility through formal schooling" (Yosso, T. 2005. p.70). Using this, the Head of Department, saw this as a transaction as opposed to helping a student who should be progressing. This form of exploitation, where she used Sabiti potentially for personal gain, also made me as an English teacher seem incompetent as she made it seem that I could not bring Sabiti through to the end of her GCSEs and did not have the ability to maintain or increase her grade; even though that is what I had been doing since Sabiti was in Year 10. These "denotations are submerged and hidden in ways that are offensive" (Ladson-Billings, G, 1998, p.9) and these actions are able to take place for two main reasons:

1. **Power**: similar to how Black people were oppressed during slavery due to the power that White people had, this same power is exerted throughout education. It is used through status and whiteness. Everyone in David Lean Academy above me was White, which is problematic because the battle to tackle racism deems more difficult as White people tend to stick together to support one another and view me as the 'Angry Black Man'.
2. **Representation**: there is not enough representation in schools, meaning that the "voice of people of colour [although] required for a deep understanding of the educational system," (Ladson-Billings, G, 1998, p.14) is not being utilized to create an impact or change within the education system. With there being an unequal balance of White teachers in comparison to those who are Black, there are not enough teachers standing up for Black students and it continues to be a battle of individual teachers against the masses. This was reflective in the classroom as the Head of

Department's class was smaller and was made up with the majority being the White pupils in the year group with a small proportion of Black pupils. The workforce works against Black teachers, as Black teachers only make up 2.3% of the workforce in comparison to 91% of White teachers (Gov.uk 2021).

These two points are not only validated through my own experiences, but also through Sabiti's experiences. In order for education to change and there to become more of a balance within not only the curriculum but the basic fair treatment of students and teachers, White people need to consciously ask themselves if they are being racist but also need to reflect on their actions and become actively anti-racist. The accusation of Sabiti cheating in her exam, not only had a lack of evidence and was demotivating for a student under a lot of pressure but also raising the grade of her White counterpart further proved that the "inequality [is] so deep rooted and so large that, under current circumstances, it is a practically inevitable feature of the education system" (Gillborn, D. 2008. p.64). Furthering this, the Head of Department imparted the notion through her actions that inequality is evident and "historical advantages built through conscious discrimination in the past [and the present have] become institutionalized to such a degree that even the removal of all existing barriers cannot create a level playing field" (Gillborn, D. 2008. p.64). Sabiti, like all of the other students revised and prepared for this exam and when she had done well, her grade was reduced and her White counterpart's grade was increased, thus, creating an unequal playing field for the two students. Although this experience for Sabiti could have demotivated her, it acted as a motivational drive for her. This resilient nature is not found in all students, and the effect could be the opposite if this were to happen to other students.

9   A Trip to the Globe Theatre

For two years, due to the Coronavirus pandemic, the students in David Lean Academy were unable to go on any trips. Two years later and a trip was organised to go to The Globe Theatre to watch Julius Caesar. This particular Shakespeare production had however been produced to reflect contemporary understanding of power and how it differs depending on race. For this to be successful, the production company used a cast that was heavily Black and of ethnic minority. The organisation of the trip came from the Head of Department and Second in Charge which would have taken a few months of preparation. The trip was for Year 7 to go on, and some of Year 8 (the year group that I on a day-to-day basis was in charge of throughout the duration of the academic year).

Throughout the preparation process, there was no communication to indicate that students from my year group would be going on the trip to The Globe Theatre. Two days before, I found out from the Head of Year 7 that there was a trip organised as she asked me, "are you going to the trip on Thursday" as to which I replied, "what trip?" As a member of the English department, I was not informed that there was a trip and on the Thursday of the trip, I came to find out that I was the only member of the English Department who was not invited to the trip which was taking place over two different days. The Head of Department and Second in Charge individually invited everyone within the department except for me, they also invited White teachers from the humanities department and maths department. The only Black teacher in the English department was the only member of the English Department not invited to take an English Department trip to a production grappling directly with issues of power and race. The irony is that the Head of Department and The Second in Charge who predominantly hold the power within my department, used their power to ensure that I, the only Black teacher, would not be invited to a Shakespeare production that tackled themes of racism and power.

When the trip was over, this was the first time that I directly heard about it from the Second in Charge within my department. I stood doing my duty in the morning by the boy's toilets and she came up to me and said "Oh, we didn't invite you to the Julius Caesar trip because we know that you go home early, and we were returning to school at 5:30pm." When the Second in Charge said this to me, I looked at her and did not respond, she then walked away. The Head of Department and Second in Charge were aware that I run basketball club which runs until 5pm. Although it is true that I go home when the school day is finished, they are both aware that I do this as I had been in school from when it opens at 6am. In dispute of her excuse, as those in charge, they should not have used their power to make the decision for me as to if I could or could not make the trip, they could have simply asked me as that was a decision that I should have been entitled to make.

10 A Trip to the Globe Theatre Analysis

Throughout my time at David Lean Academy, I have come to find that there are problematic elements when teaching Shakespeare's texts. The problem in itself does not solely sit with the texts, but it is the racism that lies within the texts without the proper teaching of context – especially to Black students. As the only Black teacher within the department, when we as a department had to teach *Othello* in 2020, I had some major problems with digesting some of the racist slurs such as "old Black ram" (*Othello* Act 1 Scene 1) and "far more fair than Black" (*Othello* Act 1 Scene 3). I openly expressed the problems with the Shakespeare text within a department meeting, whereby I was the only person in the meeting that had an outright problem with the racial slurs. All of the White teachers were nonchalant about the text and didn't see the major problems in the text. Teachers as a counterargument to the racial slurs in the text, would often question the other themes within the text and would often ask "why are we focusing only on race? What about gender? Why not class?" (Ladson-Billings, G, 1998, p.7). Gender and the treatment of women became the talking point above the racial elements within the text due to the misdirection created by the Head of Department and Second in Charge. As the two people in charge were both White female teachers, the notion of sympathy towards the racial elements as a Black teacher in a Black school was abandoned and gender alongside the mistreatment of women became the talking point. As a Black male English practitioner in dispute with a White department, it was clear that "we are not allowed to enter discourse, because we are often disqualified and excluded from it" (Yosso, T. 2005. p.69). The absurdity within this was that this text was being taught to predominantly Black students and although "Shakespeare [is deemed as] a symbol of high culture" (Balinska-Ourdeva, Johnston, Mangat & McKeown, 2014, p.337) the question at hand would be whose culture? This being said, the "cultural issues posed barriers to [students'] understanding of [the depths of the text]" (Balinska-Ourdeva, Johnston, Mangat & McKeown, 2014, p. 337) because a White text was being taught to a Black group of students whereby these students were placed in a situation where they had to read these racial slurs about the colour of their skin, and I was the only person in the department that had a real issue with this. I by no means was arguing that the text should be completely withdrawn from the David Lean Academy English curriculum, but my argument was that in order to read this with students, we need to take a sensitive approach and spend a good amount of time teaching things such as context and the surrounding issues during Shakespeare's era, which being a pre-capitalist era has a different understanding of race and otherness.

The following year, *Othello* was taken out of the curriculum. This could have been due to my expressing of extreme discomfort, or it could have been because those in charge did not like how gender was represented – nonetheless it was taken out. When the exclusion from The Globe Theatre trip occurred, the reasoning given as to why I was not invited had no correlation to me not feeling comfortable with specific Shakespeare texts and the context surrounding it, the reasoning was completely disconnected to Shakespeare in itself. The production company at Shakespeare's Globe was a company that explicitly wanted to look at Shakespeare plays from different perspectives, and they understood that "the danger lies in attempting to deal with oppression purely from a theoretical base" (Yosso, T. 2005. p.73) meaning that they would often switch the race, class or gender of the characters in their productions and seeing as Shakespeare is, "so deeply embedded in our cultural memory," (Leveen, 2017, p.5) they wanted to look at Shakespeare from an alternative, culturally relevant perspective. Seeing a production as a Black child would have allowed perspectives to be changed in relation to Shakespeare and possibly as a Black teacher this could have changed some of my perceptions on Shakespeare too, which would have ultimately allowed me to "[reflect] on the nature of literature itself." (Schaufele, 2019, p.147)

Not including me as a teacher, made me realise that the Head of Department and the Second in Charge, were possibly threatened by my outspoken attitude towards *Othello* and inviting me to The Globe Theatre, they would have been placing themselves in a position which would have made them vulnerable if I had something to say about how Black people are represented in the play. This indicated to me that there are consequences for being outspoken as a Black teacher. This form of oppression may not have "seem[ed] like oppression to the perpetrator," (Ladson-Billings, G, 1998, p.14) however this was one of the highest forms of oppression as they deliberately excluded me from something to silence my voice. This institutional racism is similar to colonialism, whereby there is full control of the curriculum without the input from the only Black teacher, and those in charge can disqualify me from trips in order to silence my voice, but "not listening to the lived experiences and histories of those oppressed by institutionalized racism" (Yosso, T. 2005. p.71) is a dangerous entity, especially when dealing with people of Black heritage. This attack on me was a mechanism to control how much input I have; it was a mechanism put in place to assert authority, thus, adding to the oppression which I have faced in the public education sector.

11   Struggles

Becoming a Middle Leader had me face subtle forms of racism throughout the academic year. As I became the Head of Year 8, I was excited about the prospect of instilling knowledge and life lessons amongst the young people. At the beginning of the school year, when receiving my teaching timetable, I stopped and counted all the hours which I had to teach. In total, there were 23 hours. I wondered how I would be able to manage a whole year group at the same time as teach such a high number of hours. For three weeks, I was unable to move into the Key Stage 3 office as there was not a desk, computer, or telephone available for me, this however was not the case for the Head of Year 7 - Samantha, and the Head of Year 9 – Greg. As the only Black Head of Year, I had to go to different classrooms which were available for the first three weeks to make phone calls to parents and take meetings. Eventually, when a desk was placed in the office, myself, Greg and Samantha were speaking about the number of hours we had all received. I was surprised that Greg had only received 18 teaching hours and Samantha 17 teaching hours. I decided to speak to the Headteacher to see if my hours could be adjusted, this was not granted.

      In this meeting with the Headteacher, I was informed that how I dressed was "tacky" and "inappropriate". For context, I wear suit trousers, shoes, and a turtleneck jumper. White teachers within the school wear chinos, turtlenecks, short skirts, belly tops and open toe heels, however my dress was "inappropriate". After this meeting, it was clear that my hours were not going to change, and I had to try my best throughout the school year with a lack of support. Although this was the case, I attempted to make the lessons as engaging as possible for students and still incorporated rap within my lessons.

Throughout the academic year, students would rave about "Mr. Asare's lessons" and would show teachers and other students raps which they had produced in my classroom. When being presented the task to complete a dissertation to do for my master's degree, it seemed purposeful to cover the original title: "Rap music in the English classroom and the impact of conversation to nurture the love of English amongst students." Correctly, University College London requires master's students to complete an ethics form and to speak to those in charge about the projects which we wanted to partake in. When initially approaching the Headteacher to see if he would allow this research to take place, he said "I have no say, you have to speak to your Head of Department." Following his direction, I prepared all the necessary paperwork to present to the Head of Department, alongside a brief on my research idea and to get permission to explore it for the remainder of the academic year. This followed a very clear plan which was outlined to the Head of Department, however I received the answer "The rap thing is great but, no." There was no reasoning given, the request to do the research was rejected. This felt like there was a personal agenda to it, one whereby her aims were to place me in a difficult situation, as she is someone who is also embarking on her master's degree so understands the pressures and work that it takes to think through these projects. I was rejected because of my relationship with students, because I was Black and also because she as an English practitioner did not understand the genre of rap or its impact on students from Black backgrounds. With her attempts to slow me down and her insecurities about me doing a degree in English Education, I believe she also felt threatened that I would go down such an educational route. In a similar way that my Headteacher at Robert Baron School did not want me to rap, my Head of Department did not want me to explore rap amongst the students or want the students rapping, even if it was about canonical texts written by racist White men.

    I think back to my journey and experiences and realise that there are many occasions whereby rap has been deemed as an 'evil' or 'violent' genre, however this is a stereotype, the stigma of which it is difficult to break. I however believe that teachers around the world, should give children chances, the same way that Mr Clemshaw gave me a chance to write and express lyrics in a poetic form which coincides with the education system. Rap can work hand in hand with education, and as soon as the system realises this, education taught to students can be more fruitful.

12 Discussion

Throughout my findings, it is extremely evident that racism comes in both "Macro and micro-forms of oppression," (Yosso, T. 2005. p.77) as there are times where White people are conscious of their oppressive actions and times where they are subconsciously racist without explicitly meaning to be. In a predominantly White sector, whereby the teachers tend to come from middle class backgrounds, it is important that there is representation in the classrooms, especially when the students may be predominantly Black, it is vital that we as Black practitioners are not "left out of the dialogue about how best to educate children of colour" (Ladson-Billings, G, 1998, p.14). Our lived experiences of when we were children and the racism we might have faced can act as a learning point and pillar for both children and teachers in the education sector. With more Black teachers in the English classroom, "there comes a moment in every class where we have to discuss "the Black Issue" and what's appropriate education for Black Children," (Ladson-Billings, G, 1998, p.14) this appropriated conversation does not only have to be with children, but it has to be with those in charge, even if you are placed in discomfortable positions when doing so. Moreover, it is equally important that schools that have a high White population of students have Black teachers to share their lived experiences; thus, opening minds to see different perspectives and for these teachers not to diminish texts but to point out the inequality throughout the process, later allowing White students and teachers to advocate against racism and the unequal treatment of Black people through their own affinity.

Being in education as a Black English teacher, whereby you are constantly dealing with canonical texts whereby those who initially wrote these texts were predominantly of White male heritage, some of which were overtly racist, you get to a stage where you become "tired of arguing with those White people" (Ladson-Billings, G, 1998, p.14). These constant battles for equality are not only draining but need to formulate into more proactive steps so that these are not *only arguments,* but they are active steps in changing the curriculum. This can only be done through diversifying teaching staff, who will advocate for a change in curriculum and have an open viewpoint of new teaching methods which will enhance Black students' experiences through cultural capital. Those within education must ensure that the "value that White people place on their own skins" (Ladson-Billings, G, 1998, p.15) is equivalent to that of Black skin and they understand that there should be equality in not only what is taught but also the conversations whereby experiences are shared. These experiences need to be taken seriously and as educators, we need to be able to openly "[understand] the saliency of race in education and the society, and it underscores the need to make racism explicit so that students can recognize and struggle against this particular form of oppression." (Ladson-Billings, G, 1998, p.19) this is significant for not explicitly Black students but all students as oppression needs to be noticed from all individuals so that they can support and fight oppression together.

"Most [Black British people] suffer the consequences of systematic and structural racism." (Ladson-Billings, G, 1998, p.20) this racism is however not exclusive to when you become an adult and begin working, this process begins when you are a child, just like my experiences in Primary School. The system is not designed in a way to help all progress, it is designed so that those of ethnic backgrounds, Black people

Discussion

specifically, are marginalised and oppressed so that they do not have the same opportunities as White people. These "consequences of systematic and structural racism" (Ladson-Billings, G, 1998, p.20) take an emotional toll on Black people and the fight becomes an unbearable and draining fight, one which many Black people are not willing to partake in as conversations consistently fall on deaf ears. Systematic racism has become most evident when entering the field of education as a teacher. We teach students about many canonical texts, however there is an importance in active steps to widen the English curriculum, this can be done through educated conversations which have proactive steps and a wider scope of texts which deem important and have memorable lessons for Black students. Ultimately, these texts need to be insightful, because "how can students be expected to deconstruct rights, "in a world with no rights" (Williams, 1995, P.98 and Ladson-Billings, G, 1998, p.16). The differences between races, class and culture needs to be explicitly explained to children and unfortunately, Black children need to work twice as hard as their White counterparts due to not only their skin colour but often their socioeconomical background. This conversation in relation to Black students and their lived experiences growing up, coinciding with my own lived experiences and current experiences as an English teacher in a Black school, surrounded by White teachers is an important conversation that many more people should have and "if we are serious about solving these problems in schools and classrooms, we have to be serious about intense study and careful rethinking of race and education," (Ladson-Billings, G, 1998, p.22) which starts through these dialogues and proactive steps that need to be overtly spoken about.

   There were many factors that occurred in this research and many experiences which I have been able to share, however I struggled to make sense of the complexity of these issues in all of the chapters although they are all intersectional. Throughout this, I have realised that there is a strong importance in not only representation, but also human

Discussion

connection as lived experiences are shared. These lived experiences need to continue to be shared as the system tries to keep people apart from one another and attempts to negate from these lived experiences and its importance. Although there are consequences for being open with students and teachers, as discrimination becomes more evident, these shared experiences are relevant and "White scholars have expanded CRT with WhiteCrit, by 'looking behind the mirror' to expose White privilege and challenge racism" (Delgado, R & Stefancic, J. 1997 & Yosso, T. 2005. p.72). Although this is very helpful and I argue that White people need to be reflective of their actions and that there is a need for everyone to work together, there is a strong need for more Black scholars and Black teachers, especially in the United Kingdom, so that they can give their perspective and real-life experiences which creates a wider array of experiences from those who are oppressed and underrepresented. These experiences will act as an aid for others going through similar situations and creates validity in first-hand experience; and through this, "we will have to expose racism in education and propose radical solutions for addressing it." (Ladson-Billings, G, 1998, p.22) which is one of the only ways that racism within education will change dramatically.

Appendix

Research proposal[10]

Title: Music in the English classroom and the impact of conversation to nurture the love of English amongst students.

It is worth mentioning that the following proposal is exclusive to my English classroom, and many may have similar experiences when dealing with their own inner city London school. There are two elements that I would like to cover in my research and these elements are linked. I will begin talking about the conversational element in the classroom and then move onto music in the English classroom.

As learning is complex and interactive, upon my thought process, I decided that my research will be cover elements of how powerful conversation could be in the English classroom and how these conversations encourage the understanding of concepts and topics. When I was in school, often, the teacher would explain a topic and then we as students were asked to proceed with a writing task. The writing tasks we were given didn't often challenge or stretch us and they were more of a tick box exercise, where I was regurgitating the topic explained. As important as writing tasks may deem to be and

---

[10] I was unable to carry out my original research design, but the proposal is included here to satisfy the requirements of the reader.

as much as education may have developed since I was in school, in this process, there was no pathway for peer learning through conversation, debates or extensive explanations from teachers that interconnected the topic at hand with real life. Writing tasks are valuable, however there is value when a teacher could give real life examples of the concepts being taught. As this was never done, I never fully grasped the rationale behind why we learnt particular texts. As a teacher, I am constantly asked in the English classroom "why are we learning this?" or being told, "I already know how to speak English" these utterances have forced me to create a rationale for why students are learning the topics at hand and what relevance it has to their lives; more importantly, why am I as a teacher teaching the topics at hand (besides the hierarchical instructions).

Through conversation, real life examples and scenarios, I am able to give clear rationales for learning specific topics, but also engage students through personal stories to help them grasp notions with much more clarity. As a student, if I had been exposed to some of the conversations that I have with my students when I was younger, I would have left school with a wider love and understanding of the relevance of English. I would have left school with a wider understanding of life and the practicalities of it and how some of the topics relate to everyday life. These conversations would have nurtured my love for English and would have allowed me to self-explore different texts. Doing more peer group exercises with a carefully thought out seating plan would have broadened my view – the same way it broadens my students' views and are able to learn from one another through paired activities. These conversations and paired activities are a great foundation for not only the classroom, but when students move on to their post 16 lives, as they will have an understanding on how to interact with others and be open to different opinions and viewpoints. Many teachers argue that their lives are private, which I do respect and agree, however the relevance of conversation is vital for students. Myself as a teacher in

Appendix

Brixton have many relatable experiences to the children, but for those who grew up in a completely different area, it is more vital that the conversations in relation to experience are expressed as students need to be exposed to different experiences other than the ones that they know.

Through this research process, there are multiple ethical issues which I must consider. One of these ethical dimensions is that I need to record some of the lessons that take place to get a grasp of the depth of conversations and what the students are gaining from these conversations. This would require students to permit me to do this. The transparency of why the recordings would take place would also need to be very clear for the students to understand, and as many of them are quite infatuated with the stories told and my adult life in general, I don't believe there will be a big issue as long as identities remain anonymous, and pseudonyms are used in the writing. A smaller problem which may occur in this process may be the presence of a camera; students may see a camera and decide that they are going to act differently to how they normally do, so the familiarity of the camera in the classroom would be important before undertaking any recording. If a camera cannot be used, then a dictaphone that is strong enough to pick up the sounds of students will suffice as I am familiar with student voices. In addition to the recording, besides formulating relevant transcripts, I would like to hold both one to one interviews (with selected students) and a small grouped interview. The purpose of holding both interviews is that I do not want answers from a grouped interview to influence opinions, so there will be value in holding the one to one interviews. The range of interviews will range from different types of students within the classroom alongside different ethnic backgrounds, however the research will be conducted with one class in Year 9. Some of the reading that will inform my writing would also cover the link between multimodality and explanatory conversation and I would like to discover how the two are interlinked alongside its effectiveness.

When I was in school, there weren't many creative

opportunities in the English classroom unless it was writing stories and there isn't much difference in the school that I am currently teaching in. The school which I teach in is an extremely academically orientated environment, however their view of academics and my view are completely juxtaposed. The school has a very strict and narrow way of teaching English, one which I as a teacher cannot completely adhere to. When given the creative writing segment to cover with students, we were advised to talk about language and structure devices, and have the students writing a story about a given topic for a minimum of 30 minutes. My problem with reducing students to a particular box or topic when dealing with creative writing in the first instance is that the element of 'creativity' becomes non-existent and they are simply writing about what they are told to write about. If it was truly creative writing, students would be allowed to write about whatever they want for at least a few lessons. When teaching creative writing I decided that I would get students to write but with a twist. The students were instructed that they could write about absolutely anything they want, the only restriction is that they had to write for one hour to a piece of instrumental music that many would all be familiar with – the piece of music was a song from a game many of them play – Minecraft.

    Prior to teaching this class the way that the school envisioned a year earlier, the students struggled to a great degree with creative writing. They struggled to include all of the literary and structural devices that the school wanted to see in their writing. The emphasis was on students using these techniques in their writing, however the students struggled because of this. Although the techniques were exclusively taught, these techniques may have been found naturally in the creative writing pieces if the students were asked to write however they feel comfortable. If the students were able to write however they liked and then the devices were taught, the students may be able to identify where they have used any devices. The mere fact that they were taught the devices before even picking up a pen to write caused restrictions for the students as they were not thinking about the creativity, but they were thinking about the language and structure devices and how to incorporate these into their writing.

When informing Year 10 and 11 students that they would be doing creative writing, the collective response from the class was a massive *sigh*, as it is not something that they have found engaging in the past. These strategies used are not only for KS4 classes but can also be used effectively for KS3 classes also. After putting the music on and giving the students clear instructions of the process which must be undertaken for the activity to be successful, the students were able to write without stopping. Throughout the research, I will speak about the process, which was carefully planned out which included:

1. Picking the music
2. Listening to the music
3. Planning their story
4. Writing their story

I will detail in the dissertation the full steps which were taken when creating this task and explain how the music was picked through a conversation with a year 7 student. An observation when this task was happening was that the students who are the most 'disengaged' were extremely engaged and were able to write for the full hour without stopping. When asking students after the task was completed if they had found it easy or difficult, to my surprise only one student in the full class found the activity difficult. The sounds of the music created ideas in the students' heads and allowed them to get creative through the exercise.

Throughout my research, I will also be writing about the benefits that rap has in the English classroom and talk about what impact this has on students from my inner-city London school. I would like to research and explore how impactful this is amongst other students in the city. I will talk on how rhythm and music can be used to teach poetry and how it can also be used as a technique when revising. I will explore the relevance of music as a whole in the classroom and how it relates to

Appendix

popular classroom culture. I will explore how it can be used for virtually anything from writing about Martin Luther King, to teaching similes and metaphors. I will speak on how students love creating raps in relation to their topics and how they create their own lyrics in their own time about specific topics being taught. I will also talk about the poetry taught in schools and why this is somewhat problematic as there is no true representation and how rapper songs like DMX's '*Innocent Man*' lyrics alongside Tupac's '*Thugz Mansion*' lyrics have been more impactful in the classroom for students when trying to understand poetry and its purpose. As this is research based, my conclusions will be informed by what I see, alongside the impact it has and student involvement. I will use samples of student work to explore if tasks were completely understood and what impact if any this had on students in the classroom. This section heavily relates to the conversational element earlier mentioned, so the two should not be treated as separate entities as they work hand in hand for this research.

Some of the readings I will use:

Britton, J. (1987). Vygotsky's contribution to pedagogical theory. English in Education. Pages 23, 25 & 26.

Golding, W (1954). Lord of the Flies.

Grainger, T. Goouch, K & Lambirth, A. (2005) Creativity and Writing: developing voice and verve in the classroom. London & New York: Routledge. Pages 122, 131, 133 & 137.

Kelly, L (2013) The English Journal Vol. 102, No. 5, Hip Hop Literature: The politics, Poetics, and Power of Hip-Hop in the English Classroom. Pages 52, 53, 54

Shelby-Caffey, C. Byfield, L & Solbrig, S. (2018) Changing English, Studies in Culture and Education Vol.25, No. 1: From Rhymes to Resistance: Hip Hop as a Critical Lens in promoting socially just teaching. Pages 72 & 74

  Although these are some of the readings which I will

explore, I will also be researching readings that relate to conversation in the classroom alongside relationships in the classroom, as conversation and relationships work hand in hand. This will allow me to make an informed decision on the impact that music and conversation has in classrooms, especially in schools whereby this is frowned upon.

Malik's rap

Our whole family suffering and Walter thinks its funny,
This the reason why I didn't tell him I have a baby in my tummy,
I want to buy a house with the 10k cheque,
Walters at the bar tryna place some bets,
Our family is poor I cant give 50 cent,
Travis said hes for gratness and that's what he ment,
Walter hates when I mention we are poor,
Thats why he gave Travis 1 Dollar when he walk through the door,
I andmite (*admit*) Walter failing as a man
Mama know she should give him a ban.
Benatha don't belive in God so im failing as a mum,
This is because im dumb,
She wants to be a doctor so god for her,
How can that be when our house im made out of fur,
I feel sorry for Walter, Travis, Benetha and the baby,
I wish Walter never laid me.

Bibliography

Balinska-Ourdeva, V., Johnston, I., Mangat, J. and McKeown, B. (2014). "What Say these Young Ones": Students' Responses to Shakespeare—An Icon of Englishness. Interchange, 44(3-4), **Page 337**

Boylorn, M, Holman Jones, S, E. Adams, T, Ellis, C (2013) Handbook of Autoethnography – "Sit With Your Legs Closed!" and Other Sayin's from My Childhood. *Left Coast Press, Inc.* Chapter 7 **Pages 173-185.**

British Dyslexia Association (2022) Retrieved from https://www.bdadyslexia.org.uk/advice/children/music-and-dyslexia Child- Music and Dyslexia Accessed on 21st August 2022

Britton, J. (1987). Vygotsky's Contribution to Pedagogical Theory. English in Education, 21(3), **pages 23-25.**

Cantwell, J. (2014). Constructing Macbeth: Text and Framing in a Secondary Urban Classroom. Changing English, 21(1), **Pages 24 – 25.**

Chawla, D, Holman Jones, S, E. Adams, T, Ellis, C (2013) Handbook of Autoethnography – Walk, Walking, Talking, Home. *Left Coast Press, Inc.* Chapter 6 **Pages 162-172.**

Bibliography

Davies, N. L. (2000). Learning ... the beat goes on. Childhood Education, 7(3). **Pages 148-153.**

Delgado, R & Stefancic, J. (Eds) (1997) *Critical white studies: looking behind the mirror* (Philadelphia, Temple University Press).

DuBois, W. E. B (1989) *The soul of black folks* (New York, Bantam). (Originally published 1903).

Dyslexia Help. (2015). Debunking the myths about dyslexia. Retrieved from http://dyslexiahelp.umich.edu/dyslexics/%20learn-about-dyslexia/what-is-dyslexia/debunking-common-myths-about-dyslexia

Eunice Kennedy Shriver National Institute of Child Health and Human Development. (2001). Put reading first: The research building blocks for teaching children to read. Washington, DC: U.S. Government Printing Office.

Gillborn, D. (2008). Racism and Education coincidence or conspiracy? *Routledge Taylor & Francis Group London and New York.* **Pages 28, 61 and 64.**

Gov.uk. Ethnicity Facts and Figures (2021) https://www.ethnicity-facts-figures.service.gov.uk/workforce-and-business/workforce-diversity/school-teacher-workforce/latest accessed on 6th August 2022.

Gov.uk. Teachers' Standards (2021) https://www.gov.uk/government/publications/teachers-standards accessed 21st August 2022.

Grainger, T. Goouch, K & Lambirth, A. (2005) Creativity and Writing: developing voice and verve in the classroom. *London & New York: Routledge.* **Page 131.**

Hansberry, L. (1959) "*A Raisin in the Sun*". First edition publication: Random House. **Whole text**

Ladson-Billings, G. (1998). Just what is critical race theory and what's it doing in a nice field like education? *International Journal of Qualitative Studies in Education.* **Pages 7 – 22.**

Leveen, L. (2017). Putting the "where" into "wherefore art thou": Urban Architectures of Desire in Romeo and Juliet. Shakespeare, 13(2), **page 5**.

Lewis, C. 2009. The Truth Behind Hip Hop. [DVD].

Mitchell, C & Jordan, F. 2004. Hope. Twista & Faith Evans. [CD]. Hollywood California: *Capitol Records*

Morrison, M & Simmons, E. 2002. Innocent Man. Mark Morrison & DMX. [CD]. California: *Death Row Records*

Pilgrim, J. (2015) Hitting the Right "Note": Using music to promote fluency skills for dyslexic students. A Journal of the Texas Council of Teachers of English Language Arts - Inquiries and innovations – Recording the past and composing the future. *English in Texas Volume 45.1.* **Pages 15 -18.**

Register, D. (2001). The effects of an early intervention music curriculum on prereading/writing. Journal of Music Therapy, 38(3) **pages 239-248.**

Schaufele, M. (2019). Why Are We Reading This? Hermeneutic Inquiry into the Practice of Teaching (with) Literature. Educational Studies, 56(2) **page 147.**

Shakespeare, W. (2018). Othello. London: Bloomsbury Arden Shakespeare

Shakur, T. & Jones, N. 2002. Thugz Mansion. Tupac Shakur & Nas. [CD]. California: Marin City: *Amaru Entertainment*

Shelby-Caffey, C. Byfield, L & Solbrig, S. (2018) Changing English, Studies in Culture and Education Vol.25, No. 1: From Rhymes to Resistance: Hip Hop as a Critical Lens in promoting socially just teaching. **Page 72.**

Sumara, D.J. (2002). Why reading literature in school still matters imagination, interpretation, insight. *New York; London Routledge Taylor And Francis Group* **Page 157.**

Texas Scottish Rite Hospital for Children. (n.d.). Dyslexia. Retrieved from http://www.tsrhc.org/dyslexia

Texas Scottish Rite Hospital for Children. (2014). Dyslexia defined. Retrieved from http://www.tsrhc.org/TSRHC/media/Media/Library-Files/PDF/Dyslexia-Defined-2015-links_3.pdf

Turvey, A., Brady, M., Carpenter, A. and Yandell, J. (2006). The many voices of the English classroom. English in Education, 40(1), **Page 59.**

Washburn, E. K., Joshi, R. M., & Binks-Cantrell, E. S. (2011). Teacher knowledge of basic language concepts and dyslexia. Dyslexia, 17(2). **Pages 165-183.**

Weems, M, Holman Jones, S, E. Adams, T, Ellis, C (2013) Handbook of Autoethnography – Fire A Year in Poems. *Left Coast Press, Inc.* Chapter 15 **Pages 313-320.**

Williams, P. (1995). Alchemical notes: Reconstructing ideals from deconstructed rights. In R. Delgado (Ed.), Critical race theory: the cutting edge. *MA: Harvard University Press.* **Page 98.**

Yosso, T. (2005). Whose culture has capital? A critical race theory discussion of community cultural wealth. *Race Ethnicity and Education.* **Pages 69 – 77.**